rosen publishing's
rosen central®
New York

Dr. Kim Chilman-Blair and John Taddeo
Medical content reviewed for accuracy by Dr. Vas Novelli and Dr. Karyn Moshal

This edition published in 2011 by:

The Rosen Publishing Group, Inc.
29 East 21st Street
New York, NY 10010

Additional end matter copyright © 2011 by The Rosen Publishing Group, Inc.

Library of Congress Cataloging-in-Publication Data

Chilman-Blair, Kim.
 Medikidz explain HIV / Kim Chilman-Blair and John Taddeo ; medical content reviewed for accuracy by Vas Novelli and Karyn Moshal.
       p. cm. -- (Superheroes on a medical mission)
 Includes bibliographical references and index.
 ISBN 978-1-4358-9458-7 (library binding) -- ISBN 978-1-4488-1839-6 (pbk.) -- ISBN 978-1-4488-1840-2 (6-pack)
 1. AIDS (Disease)--Comic books, strips, etc.--Juvenile literature. 2. HIV (Viruses)--Comic books, strips, etc.--Juvenile literature. I. Taddeo, John. II. Title.
 QR201.A37C55 2011
 614.5'993900207--dc22
                                2010001333

Manufactured in China

CPSIA Compliance Information: Batch #MS0102YA: For further information, contact Rosen Publishing, New York, New York, at 1-800-237-9932.

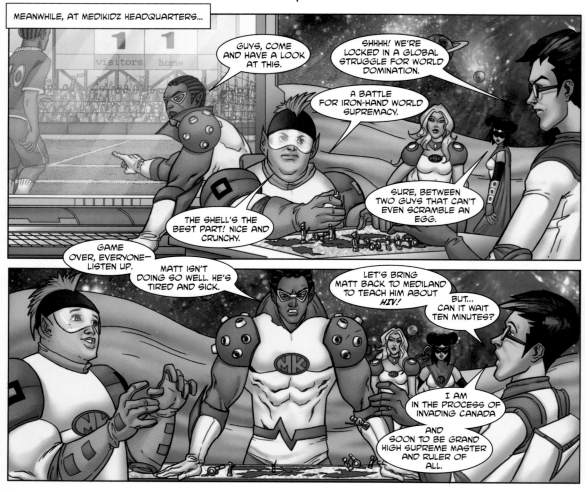

THE FLU VIRUS

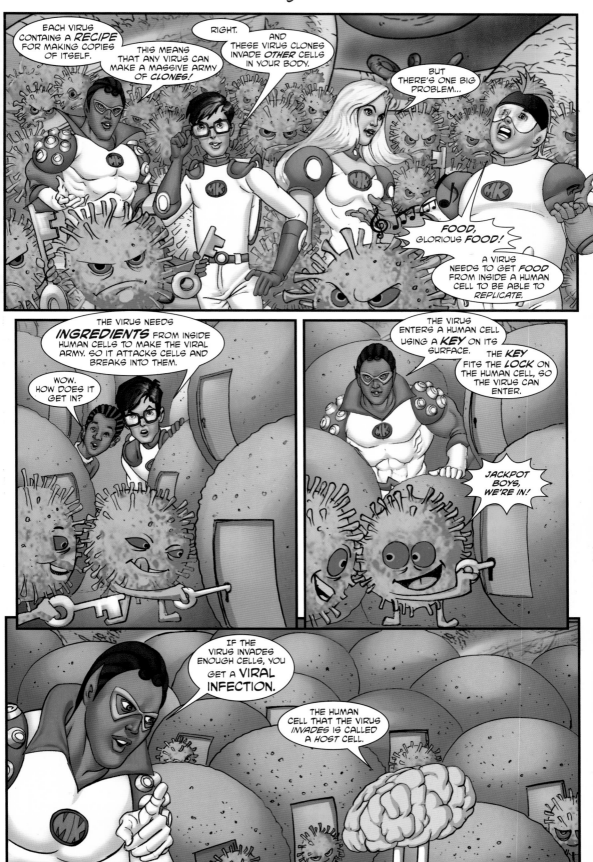

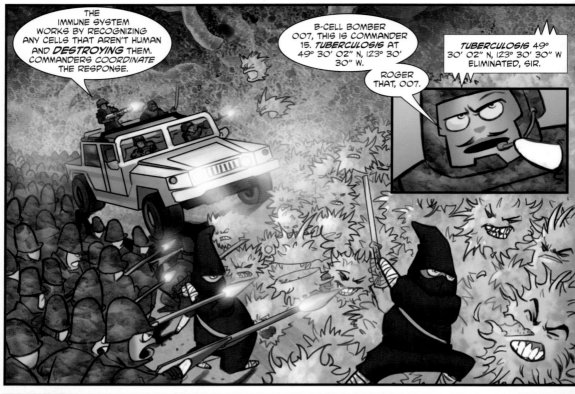

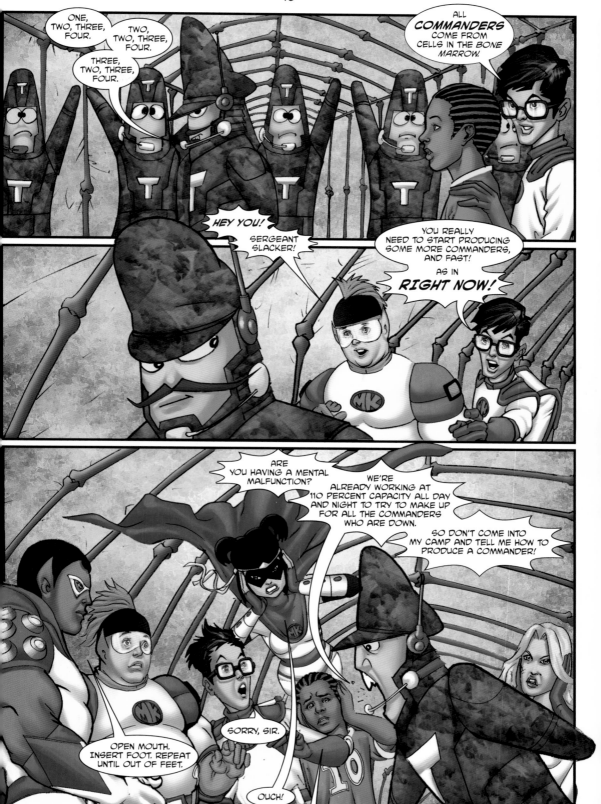

IT APPEARS THEY ARE MAKING THEM AS QUICKLY AS POSSIBLE.
BUT WE NEED MORE COMMANDERS!
THE HIV VIRUS IS DESTROYING THEM AT A RAPID RATE,
EVEN FASTER THAN YOUR BODY CAN MAKE NEW, HEALTHY ONES.
BUT THAT MEANS THAT THE NINJAS, SOLDIERS, AND BOMBERS WILL ALL BE SITTING AROUND WAITING FOR COMMANDS THAT WILL NEVER COME AND EVERY FUNGUS, BACTERIUM, AND VIRUS WILL BE ABLE TO—
OH NO!
ARE YOU TELLING ME THAT THE BODY IS LEFT UNPROTECTED?
I'M AFRAID SO, MATT.
WITH NO ONE AROUND TO COORDINATE YOUR BODY'S NATURAL ARMY...
WELL, YOU CAN SEE FOR YOURSELF...

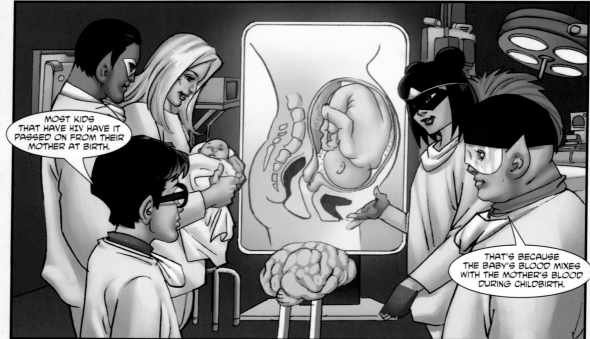

GLOSSARY

ANTIBODIES PROTECTIVE PROTEINS MADE BY A PERSON'S
    WHITE BLOOD CELLS TO FIGHT INFECTIONS.
BACTERIA (SINGULAR, BACTERIUM) MICROSCOPIC SINGLE-
    CELL ORGANISMS, SOME OF WHICH CAN CAUSE
    DISEASES.
B-CELLS WHITE BLOOD CELL LYMPHOCYTES, FORMED IN
    BONE MARROW IN MAMMALS AND PRESENT IN BLOOD
    AND LYMPH, THAT CREATE ANTIBODIES IN RESPONSE
    TO VIRUSES, BACTERIA, OR FUNGI.
BLOOD TRANSFUSION THE TRANSFER OF BLOOD OR
    BLOOD PROJECTS FROM ONE PERSON TO ANOTHER.
CD4 PROTEIN A PROTEIN THAT IS MOSTLY FOUND ON
    THE SURFACE OF HELPER T-CELLS; IN HUMANS, IT IS A
    RECEPTOR FOR HIV, ENABLING THE VIRUS TO GAIN
    ENTRY INTO ITS HOST.
CHICKEN POX A HIGHLY INFECTIOUS VIRAL DISEASE,
    ESPECIALLY AFFECTING CHILDREN, CHARACTERIZED BY
    A RASH OF SMALL ITCHING BLISTERS ON THE SKIN
    AND A MILD FEVER.
CHRONIC CONTINUING FOR A LONG TIME OR HAPPENING
    FREQUENTLY.
CLONE A COLLECTION OF ORGANISMS OR CELLS THAT ARE
    GENETICALLY IDENTICAL.
COMMON COLD A VIRAL INFECTION OF THE NOSE
    AND THROAT, CHARACTERIZED BY SNEEZING, NASAL
    CONGESTION, COUGHING, AND HEADACHE.
FLU A WIDESPREAD VIRAL ILLNESS THAT PRODUCES
    A HIGH TEMPERATURE, SORE THROAT, RUNNY NOSE,
    HEADACHE, DRY COUGH, AND MUSCLE PAIN.
FUNGI (SINGULAR, FUNGUS) SPORE-PRODUCING
    ORGANISMS, SUCH AS MILDEWS AND MOLDS, THAT
    LIVE BY ABSORBING NUTRIENTS FROM ORGANIC
    MATTER.
HIV HUMAN IMMUNODEFICIENCY VIRUS; THE VIRUS THAT
    CAUSES AIDS.
HOST CELL A CELL THAT SUPPORTS A PARASITE, AN
    ORGANISM THAT FEEDS ON CELLS, TISSUES, OR
    FLUIDS OF ANOTHER LIVING ORGANISM (THE HOST).
IMMUNE SYSTEM A SYSTEM THAT PROTECTS THE BODY
    AGAINST DISEASE.
IMPLORE TO PLEAD WITH SOMEBODY TO DO SOMETHING.

INFECTION A DISEASE THAT IS CATCHING; AN INFECTING
      MICROORGANISM.
INVADE TO ENTER OR SPREAD THROUGH SOMETHING.
LYMPHOCYTE A WHITE BLOOD CELL IN THE IMMUNE SYSTEM
      THAT PRODUCES ANTIBODIES TO ATTACK INFECTED
      AND CANCEROUS CELLS, AND IS RESPONSIBLE FOR
      REJECTING FOREIGN TISSUE.
MEASLES A CONTAGIOUS VIRAL DISEASE WITH SYMPTOMS
      THAT INCLUDE A BRIGHT RED RASH OF SMALL SPOTS
      THAT SPREAD TO COVER THE WHOLE BODY.
NEUTROPHIL THE MOST COMMON TYPE OF WHITE BLOOD
      CELL IN VERTEBRATES, RESPONSIBLE FOR
      PROTECTING THE BODY AGAINST INFECTION.
OPPORTUNISTIC INFECTION AN INFECTION THAT OCCURS
      WHEN ORGANISMS TAKE ADVANTAGE OF A
      WEAKENED IMMUNE SYSTEM.
PARASITE AN ORGANISM THAT LIVES ON ANOTHER, A
      HOST ORGANISM, IN A WAY THAT HARMS THE HOST.
REPLICATE TO REPRODUCE EXACTLY AN ORGANISM OR A
      CELL.
RESUSCITATE TO REVIVE SOMEBODY.
RETROVIRUS A VIRUS THAT REPRODUCES IN THE BODY BY
      REPLICATING WITHIN THE BODY'S DNA.
T-CELL THE TYPE OF WHITE BLOOD CELL THAT PRODUCES
      ANTIBODIES.
TUBERCULOSIS AN INFECTIOUS DISEASE THAT CAUSES
      SMALL ROUNDED SWELLINGS TO FORM ON MUCOUS
      MEMBRANES, ESPECIALLY AFFECTING THE LUNGS.
VIRUS A TINY GERM THAT NEEDS TO ENTER THE CELLS OF
      A LIVING ORGANISM TO BECOME ACTIVATED AND
      MULTIPLY.
WHITE BLOOD CELLS CELLS THAT CIRCULATE IN THE
      BLOODSTREAM AND LYMPH SYSTEM THROUGHOUT
      THE BODY; PART OF THE IMMUNE SYSTEM THAT
      ATTACKS FOREIGN INVADERS OF THE BODY.

AIDS ALLIANCE FOR CHILDREN, YOUTH, AND FAMILIES
1600 K STREET NW, SUITE 200
WASHINGTON, DC 20006
(888) 917-2437
WEB SITE: HTTP://WWW.AIDS-ALLIANCE.ORG
THIS NONPROFIT GROUP FOCUSES ON THE CONCERNS
OF CHILDREN, YOUNG ADULTS, WOMEN, AND FAMILIES
AFFECTED BY HIV AND AIDS.

AIDS.GOV
U.S. DEPARTMENT OF HEALTH AND HUMAN SERVICES
200 INDEPENDENCE AVENUE SW
WASHINGTON, DC 20201
WEB SITE: HTTP://WWW.AIDS.GOV
THIS GOVERNMENT SERVICE PROVIDES RELIABLE
RESOURCES TO THE PUBLIC ABOUT HIV AND AIDS.

AIDSINFO
P.O. BOX 6303
ROCKVILLE, MD 20849-6303
(800) 448-0440
WEB SITE: HTTP://WWW.AIDSINFO.NIH.GOV
AIDSINFO IS A U.S. DEPARTMENT OF HEALTH AND HUMAN
SERVICES PROJECT THAT OFFERS INFORMATION ON
HIV AND AIDS TREATMENT, PREVENTION, AND
RESEARCH.

CANADIAN AIDS SOCIETY
190 O'CONNOR STREET, SUITE 800
OTTAWA, ON K2P 2R3
CANADA
(800) 499-1986
WEB SITE: HTTP://WWW.CDNAIDS.CA
THIS GROUP IS A NETWORK OF MORE THAN 100
COMMUNITY-BASED AIDS ORGANIZATIONS ACROSS
CANADA.

CANADIAN HIV/AIDS INFORMATION CENTRE
400-1565 CARLING AVENUE
OTTAWA, ON K1Z 8R1
CANADA

(877) 999-7740
WEB SITE: HTTP://WWW.AIDSSIDA.CPHA.CA
THIS CENTER IS THE LARGEST INFORMATION WAREHOUSE
    ON HIV/AIDS IN CANADA.

CENTERS FOR DISEASE CONTROL AND PREVENTION (CDC)
1600 CLIFTON ROAD
ATLANTA, GA 30333
(800) 232-6348
THE CDC IS THE NATION'S MAIN FEDERAL AGENCY FOR
    PROTECTING THE HEALTH AND SAFETY OF AMERICANS.
    IT MONITORS AND SEEKS TO CONTROL THE SPREAD
    OF DISEASES IN THE UNITED STATES.

GLOBAL NETWORK OF PEOPLE LIVING WITH HIV/AIDS
P.O. BOX 11726
1001 GS AMSTERDAM
THE NETHERLANDS
+31 20 423 4114
WEB SITE: HTTP://WWW.GNPPLUS.NET
THIS ORGANIZATION FIGHTS FOR THE RIGHTS OF PEOPLE
    LIVING WITH HIV AND AIDS.

LIFEBEAT, INC.
630 NINTH AVENUE, SUITE 1010
NEW YORK, NY 10036
(212) 459-2590
WEB SITE: HTTP://WWW.LIFEBEAT.ORG
THIS ORGANIZATION'S MISSION IS TO MOBILIZE THE
    TALENTS AND RESOURCES OF THE MUSIC INDUSTRY
    TO RAISE AWARENESS ABOUT HIV/AIDS AMONG
    YOUNG PEOPLE IN AMERICA.

WEB SITES

DUE TO THE CHANGING NATURE OF INTERNET LINKS, ROSEN
PUBLISHING HAS DEVELOPED AN ONLINE LIST OF WEB SITES
RELATED TO THE SUBJECT OF THIS BOOK. THIS SITE IS
UPDATED REGULARLY. PLEASE USE THIS LINK TO ACCESS
THE LIST:

HTTP://WWW.ROSENLINKS.COM/MED/HIV

BANISH, ROSLYN. *FOCUS ON LIVING: PORTRAITS OF AMERICANS WITH HIV AND AIDS.* AMHERST, MA: UNIVERSITY OF MASSACHUSETTS PRESS, 2003.

BARDHAN-QUALLEN, SUDIPTA. *AIDS.* DETROIT, MI: KIDHAVEN PRESS, 2005.

BARNETT, TONY, AND ALAN WHITESIDE. *AIDS IN THE TWENTY-FIRST CENTURY: DISEASE AND GLOBALIZATION.* NEW YORK, NY: PALGRAVE MACMILLAN, 2003.

CEFREY, HOLLY. *AIDS (EPIDEMICS: DEADLY DISEASES THROUGHOUT HISTORY).* NEW YORK, NY: ROSEN PUBLISHING, 2001.

CONNOLLY, SEAN. *AIDS.* CHICAGO, IL: HEINEMANN LIBRARY, 2003.

CRITZER, TIMOTHY. *HIV AND ME: FIRSTHAND INFORMATION FOR COPING WITH HIV AND AIDS.* SAN FRANCISCO, CA: FIRSTHAND BOOKS, 2004.

GELLETLY, LEEANNE. *AIDS AND HEALTH ISSUES (AFRICA: PROGRESS AND PROBLEMS).* BROOMALL, PA: MASON CREST PUBLISHERS, 2006

GRODECK, BRETT, AND DANIEL S. BERGER. *THE FIRST YEAR—HIV: AN ESSENTIAL GUIDE FOR THE NEWLY DIAGNOSED.* REV. ED. NEW YORK, NY: DA CAPO PRESS, 2007.

HALPIN, MIKKI. *IT'S YOUR WORLD—IF YOU DON'T LIKE IT, CHANGE IT: ACTIVISM FOR TEENAGERS.* NEW YORK, NY: SIMON PULSE, 2004.

KALICHMAN, SETH C., ED. *POSITIVE PREVENTION: REDUCING HIV TRANSMISSION AMONG PEOPLE LIVING WITH HIV/AIDS.* NEW YORK, NY: SPRINGER PUBLISHING, 2006.

KANE, BRIGID M. *HIV/AIDS TREATMENT DRUGS (DRUGS: THE STRAIGHT FACTS).* NEW YORK, NY: CHELSEA HOUSE PUBLISHERS, 2008.

LYON, MAUREEN E., AND LAWRENCE J. D'ANGELO, EDS. *TEENAGERS, HIV, AND AIDS: INSIGHTS FROM YOUTHS LIVING WITH THE VIRUS.* WESTPORT, CT: PRAEGER PUBLISHERS, 2006.

QUICKSAND: HIV/AIDS IN OUR LIVES. SOMERVILLE, MA: CANDLEWICK PRESS, 2009.

ROBINSON, RICHARD. *FREQUENTLY ASKED QUESTIONS ABOUT AIDS AND HIV (FAQ: TEEN LIFE).* NEW YORK, NY: ROSEN PUBLISHING, 2009.

WHITE, RYAN, ANN MARIE CUNNINGHAM, AND JEAN WHITE. *RYAN WHITE, MY OWN STORY.* NEW YORK, NY: SIGNET, 1992.

INDEX

ABOUT THE AUTHORS

DR. KIM CHILMAN-BLAIR IS A MEDICAL DOCTOR WITH TEN YEARS OF EXPERIENCE IN MEDICAL WRITING AND A PASSION FOR PROVIDING MEDICAL INFORMATION THAT MAKES CHILDREN WANT TO LEARN.

JOHN TADDEO, FORMALLY OF MARVEL ENTERTAINMENT, IS A CELEBRATED COMIC BOOK WRITER AND DIRECTOR OF TWO AWARD-WINNING ANIMATED SHORTS.